UNDERSTANDING GOD

Can I Trust Him?
A Mini Theology for Kids

Janine McNally

ISBN - Paperback: 979-8-9896732-6-1
Second Edition: December 2025.
Printed in the United States of America.

Janine McNally, Th. M., D. Min.
Panama City, FL 32401
Janine@EquippingFireflies.com

Dear Parents

When your child asks tough questions about God, do you have the answers? This is the third book in a seven-book series called "Understanding Life." Each book in the series uses an apologetic approach to answering the questions that children are asking today.

Questions like:

- Is the Bible Trustworthy?
- Who is God?
- Who am I?

It answers questions about who God is, what He is like, and why we should trust Him.

Parents and grandparents can participate in this discipleship process by encouraging their child or grandchild, answering their questions, and stepping in to help when needed.

I hope this book will guide you as you endeavor to fulfill your God-given command to disciple your children.

Remember:

- Pray for your child that they will grow to know Jesus

more each day.
- Don't expect your children to be perfect. Even though they may be saved, they are still sinners.
- Help them look up bible verses and write answers in their books.

The extent to which your child will apply these lessons depends largely relies on the support and encouragement you provide as a parent.

We are praying for you.

"These commandments that I give you today are to be on your hearts. **Impress** them on your children. **Talk** about them when you sit at home, when you walk along the road when you lie down, and when you get up."
Deuteronomy 6:6-7 [NIV].

Table of Contents

Page

Understanding God

I'm betting that you have questions about God. I think we've all had questions. Lots of them.

It is normal to have questions about God and what He is like.

It's never wrong to ask questions. The most important thing is knowing where to find the right answers.

Today, you can find answers to whatever question pops into your head. A quick internet search will bring up hundreds of answers. But it doesn't mean that they are GOOD answers.

Perhaps you've had many questions but haven't found any answers. That doesn't mean that there aren't answers. Keep reading, and hopefully, you will find them.

If you have questions, try to find the answers from people you trust.

- Ask your parent or a leader from your church.
- Or read a book like this.

Just remember.

1. God is not afraid of your questions.

2. Never be afraid to be honest with Him about your pain and fears.

Big Questions

1. What is God Like?

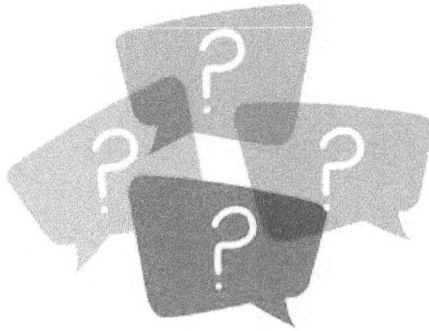

1. What is God Like?

We hear people telling us to "trust God."
But it's not easy to trust someone you cannot see.

- What does God look like?
- How do you know He's there?
- What is He like?

We don't know what God looks like. The Bible doesn't tell us.

Read this verse from the Bible.

> "**No one** has ever seen God."
> 1 John 4:12 (NIV).

Trying to see God is a bit like trying to see the wind.

You can't see the wind, but you can see its effect. You see the trees moving and the waves breaking.
But you can't see it.

We might not be able to see God, but we do know some things about Him.

The Bible says we can see God's glory and power when we look at the world around us.

UNDERSTANDING GOD

We can see God's glory when we look to the skies.

Read this verse.

> "The **heavens** declare the glory of God; the
> **skies** proclaim the work of His hands."
> Psalm 19:1 (NIV).

We can look at creation and see God's creativity.

We can see God's gentleness in the delicate petals of a flower.

Or touch the fur of soft baby bunnies.

We can see God's strength in the force of the ocean waves.

We can see His greatness when we look up to the tall, snowy mountain ranges.

We can see God's creativity in the variety of plants and animals He made.

So, we might not be able to see God, but we can know He is there. We can see the effect that He has.

- We can see creation.

- We can see how God is changing people's lives.

We can be sure of what we hope for.
We can trust in what we do not see.

Trusting what you cannot see is called "faith."

The Bible says:

> **"Faith is being sure** of what we hope for.
> **It is being sure** of what we do not see."
> Hebrews 11:1 (NIRV).

- If we KNOW something will happen, then there is no trust involved.

- If we can SEE something, there is no faith needed.

You might not be able to see God, but He sees you!
You might not be able to hear God in an audible voice, but He hears you!

The same is true with God.

We might not know what God looks like, but the Bible tells us a LOT about God.

Knowing what God is like will help you understand when you have questions.

Whether you know Jesus or are just beginning to ask questions, the Bible is the only source of truth regarding God.

1. God is Omnipresent

The first thing we know about God is that He is "omnipresent."

This is a BIG word which is made up of two smaller Latin words that have been put together.

"Omnipresent" = "Omni" + "Present."
"Omni" (means "all" or "every") + "Present."

So, "omni-present" means that God is "all-present."

God is in all places at all times.
He lives in heaven, but He is with us here on earth.

Read these verses.

> "There is no one like the Lord our God.
> **He lives in the heights** above, but **He bends down
> to see the heavens and the earth."**
> Psalm 113:5-6 (NIRV).

And God is always watching!

> "From heaven, **the LORD looks down**
> and sees all mankind."
> Psalms 33:13 (NIV).

We are never alone.

God is always present wherever we go.
He is always there.

Read these verses.

> "**Where** can I go from Your Spirit? **Where** can I flee
> from Your presence? If I go up to the heavens,
> **You are there**. If I make my bed in the depths,
> **You are there**. If I rise on the wings of the dawn,
> If I settle on the far side of the sea, **even there,**
> Your hand will guide me;
> Your right hand will hold me fast."
> Psalm 139:7-10 (NIV).

Where is God?

In the H __ __ __ __ __ __ __.

In the D __ __ __ __ __ __.

In the D __ __ __.

In the far side of the S __ __.

God is EVERYWHERE.

God promises to be with us, no matter what.

> "Do not be afraid; do not be discouraged, for **the LORD your God will be with you** wherever you go."
> Joshua 1:9 (NIV).

In the Old Testament part of the Bible, we read about a change of leadership in the nation of Israel.

Moses was old, and God named Joshua to be the man who would lead the nation across the Jordan River to the promised land.

I'm sure Joshua was afraid of what He might face as He led the way into enemy territory, but God promised that He would be right there with Joshua.

Read this verse.

> "The Lord Himself will go ahead of you. **He will be with you.** He will never leave you. **He'll never desert you.** So don't be afraid. Don't lose hope."
> Deuteronomy 31:8 (NIV).

The same promise is repeated in the New Testament.

God says:

> "I **will never leave you**. I will **never desert you**."
> Hebrews 13:5 (NIV).

God promised to be with Joshua, and God promises to be with us.

But how can God be everywhere? How is that possible?

Read these Bible verses.

> "**God is Spirit,** and His worshipers must worship in the Spirit and in Truth."
> John 4:24 (NIV).

God can be everywhere because He is a S __ __ __ __ __.

> "The Son [Jesus] is **the image of the invisible God**."
> Colossians 1:15 (NIV).

God is also I __ __ __ __ __ __ __ __.

God the Father does not have a human body.

God is not a human being like us.

> **"God is not human,** that He should lie, **not a human being,** that He should change His mind."
> Numbers 23:19 (NIV).

God is not like us.

> "Now to the King eternal, immortal, **invisible,** the only God, be honor and glory for ever and ever."
> 1 Timothy 1:17 (NIV).

God is E __ __ __ __ __. He is forever.

God is I __ __ __ __ __ __ __. He is not human.

God is I __ __ __ __ __ __ __ __ __, He cannot be seen.

We can be sure that God will be right beside us as we face whatever struggles our day might bring.

God is EVERYWHERE..

2. God is Omniscient

"Omniscient" is another big word made up of two Latin words. ("omni + scient").

> "Omni" means "All."
> "Scientia" is Latin for "knowledge."

What does the word "scient" sound like to you?
Yes – In English, we get the word "science."

So, "Omniscient" = "Omni" + "Scient."
God has "All Knowledge."

Here are some verses that teach that God knows everything before it even happens.

Read these Bible verses.

"I am God. There is no other God. I am God.
There is no one like Me.
**Before something even happens,
I announce how it will end.**
In fact, from times long ago I announced
what was still to come. I say, 'My plan will succeed.
I will do anything I want to do.'"
Isaiah 46:9-10 (NIV).

God knows before things happen.

- He decides how things will end.

- He decides what is still coming.

- His plans will always succeed, and He will do whatever He wants.

I want God on my side! Don't you?

Read these Bible verses.

> "Great is our Lord and mighty in power;
> **His understanding has no limit.**"
> Psalm 147:5 (NIV).

God U _ _ _ _ S _ _ _ _ everything.

> "If our hearts judge us, we know that God is greater than our hearts. And **He knows everything**."
> 1 John 3:20 (NIV).

God K _ _ _ _ everything.

If you create something, like a giant Lego model, you know and understand how it was all put together.

It's the same with God.

UNDERSTANDING GOD

God knows and understands everything about us.

God knows everything about yesterday, today, and tomorrow.

He knows what has happened in the past and what will happen in the future.

He knows EVERYTHING.

3. God is Omnipotent

Lastly, God is "omnipotent."
I bet you can figure out what this word means without any help.

It is also made up of two Latin words.

> "Omni" = "All"
> "Potent" = "To have great power."

The Bible teaches us that God is all-powerful. He can do anything that He wants to do. Nothing or nobody is stronger than God.

Read these Bible verses.

> "Ah, Sovereign Lord, You have made the heavens and the earth by Your great power and outstretched arm. **Nothing is too hard for You."**
> Jeremiah 32:17 (NIV).

One of the most amazing ways God showed His power was when He created everything.

God created everything from nothing.
He created light and darkness, water and sky, and sea and land.

He created the sun, moon, and stars, and plants and animals.

> "In the beginning,
> **God created the heavens and the earth**."
> Genesis 1:1 (NIV).

And best of all, He created people.

We can be sure that God can handle all of life's issues. He can defeat any enemy that we might face.

> **"He brings princes to naught** and **reduces the rulers of this world to nothing**."
> Isaiah 40:23 (NIV).

He is strong and mighty!

> "Who is the King of Glory?
> The Lord, who is **strong and mighty**.
> The Lord, who is mighty in battle."
> Psalm 24:8 (NIRV).

Our lives are safely in His hands.

> **"In His hand is the life of every creature**
> and the breath of all mankind."
> Job 12:10 (NIV).

And best of all, He promises to fight for us.

Read these Bible verses.

> "When you go to war against your enemies and see horses and chariots and an army greater than yours, do not be afraid of them, because the LORD your God, who brought you up out of Egypt, will be with you… **For the LORD your God is the one who goes with you to fight for you** against your enemies to give you victory."
> Deuteronomy 20:1,4 (NIV).

With God on our side, we cannot lose.

> "**With your help, I can advance against a troop; with my God, I can scale a wall.** As for God, His way is perfect: The LORD's word is flawless; **He shields all** who take refuge in him. **It is God who arms me with strength and keeps my way secure.**"
> 2 Samuel 22:30-31, 33 (NIV).

He is always with us. He knows everything. He is all-powerful.

God can do A __ __ T __ __ __ __.
That means that we can trust Him with our lives.

UNDERSTANDING GOD

Big Questions

1. What is God Like?
2. How Did God Create the World?

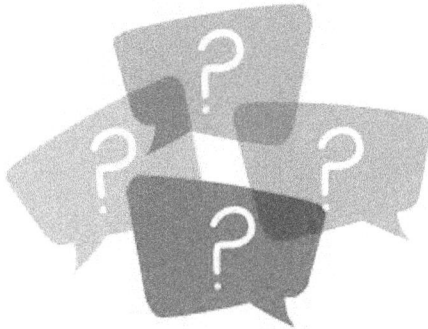

2. How Did God Create the World?

How did God create the world?

God spoke a word.

He spoke, and everything was created.

Just. Like. That!

Read this Bible verse.

> "**By the word of the Lord** the heavens were made,
> their starry host **by the breath of his mouth.**
> **For he spoke,** and it came to be;
> **He commanded,** and it stood firm."
> Psalm 33:6, 9 (NIV).

Fill in the blanks.

By the W __ __ __ of the Lord.

By the B __ __ __ __ __ of His mouth.

He S __ __ __ __, and it came to be.

He C __ __ __ __ __ __ __ __, and it stood firm.

God is so powerful; all He had to do was say the word!

God spoke all things into existence, and then He laid everything out with His hand.

Read this Bible verse.

> "**With My own hand**, I laid the foundations of the earth. **With My right hand**, I spread out the heavens."
> Isaiah 48:13 (NIRV).

God laid out everything just the way He wanted.

After that, God declared that everything He had created was "good."

And then, God created people.

Read this Bible verse.

> "God saw all that He had made, and behold, **it was VERY good!**"
> Genesis 1:31 (NIV).

After creating people, God said it was V __ __ __ good. People were God's BEST achievement.

YOU are the most special and precious part of God's creation.

Big Questions

1. What is God Like?
2. How Did God Create the World?
3. Who Created God?

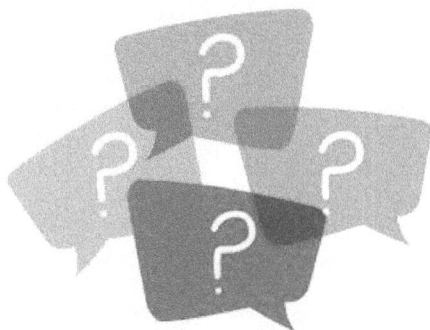

UNDERSTANDING GOD

3. Who Created God?

You might wonder, "Who created God?" Where did He come from?

The Bible tells us that:

- No one created God.
- God was never created.
- God has always just "been."

God has always existed. He created everything! He is the beginning of everything.

Nothing existed before God because He created all that exists.

Read this Bible verse.

> **"I am the Alpha and the Omega, the Beginning and the End,"** says the Lord God.
> "I am the God who is, and who was, and who will come. I am the Mighty One."
> Revelation 1:8 (NIV).

When God said that He is the Alpha and Omega, it was like saying that He is the "A" and the "Z."

Alpha is the first letter of the Greek alphabet, and Omega is the last letter.

God says that He is the B __ __ __ __ __ __ __ __

and the E __ __.

- God is the first and the last.

- He is the beginning and the end.

In other words, God was never born, nor will He get old. He has no beginning or end.

Read these Bible verses.

> "In the beginning, Lord, You laid the foundations of the earth, and the heavens are the work of Your hands. They will perish, but **You remain**... they will be changed. But You remain the same, and **Your years will never end**"
> Hebrews 1:10-12 (NIV).

So, was there anything before God?
When did God "begin?"

It's hard to imagine that God had no beginning.

- Things have to be made by someone, right?

- They can't just exist on their own, can they?

- Everything has a beginning. Doesn't it?

As hard as it is to believe, God has always been there.

No one made Him.
He has no beginning and no ending.

It's not easy to understand, but God is powerful and will always be there to take care of us!

UNDERSTANDING GOD

Big Questions

1. What is God Like?

2. How Did God Create the World?

3. Who Created God?

4. How Can Jesus Be God, But Also God's Son?

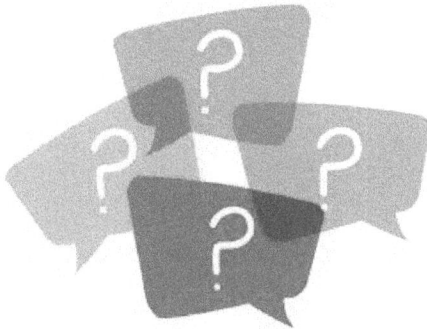

UNDERSTANDING GOD

4. How Can Jesus Be God, But Also God's Son?

If Jesus is really God, then how can He also be God's Son?

This is one of the most difficult things to understand about God.

Our brains cannot fully grasp everything there is to know about God. If we could, then we would be God.

Let's begin with what we do know!

1. There is only ONE God.

We know that the Bible teaches that there is only ONE God.

Read these Bible verses.

> "Hear, O Israel: The Lord our God, **the Lord is One**."
> Deuteronomy 6:4 (NIV).

Fill in the blanks.

The Lord is O __ __.

There is ONE God, and He is over everything.

> "**One God** and Father of all, **who is
> over all and through all and in all**."
> Ephesians 4:6 (NIV).

There is ONE God, and there is NO ONE else like Him.

> "I am God, and **there is NO other**;
> I am God, and there is **NONE like Me**."
> Isaiah 46:9 (NIV).

So far, so good.

But this is where it gets tricky!

2. God is THREE People in ONE.

Although there is only one God, the Bible teaches us that God is **THREE in ONE**.

The Bible term for this is the **"Trinity"** ("Tri-nity").

You know what "Tri" means, right?

Like a "tri-angle." THREE sides.

Or a "tri-cycle" THREE wheels.

Or a "tri-pod." THREE legs.

So, the word "Tri-nity" means a group of three.

The Bible teaches us that God is "THREE" people in "ONE."

1. God the **Father**.
2. God the **Son**.
3. God the **Holy Spirit**.

Each of them is equally God, but is also one unique Person.

We see all three Persons of the Trinity linked together in the Bible in a few places.

Read these Bible verses.

> "Therefore, go and make disciples of all nations,
> baptizing them in the name of the **Father**
> and of the **Son**
> and of the **Holy Spirit**."
> Matthew 28:19 (NIV).

Fill in the blanks.

"… in the name of the F _ _ _ _ _ and of the S _ _
and of the H _ _ _ S _ _ _ _ _ _.

> "May the grace of the **Lord Jesus Christ [the Son]**,
> and the love of **God [the Father]**, and the
> fellowship of the **Holy Spirit** be with you all."
> 2 Corinthians 13:14 (NIV).

The Holy Spirit came upon Jesus at His baptism.

> "The **Holy Spirit** came to rest on **Him [Jesus]**
> in the form of a dove. A voice **[God the Father]**
> came from heaven.
> It said, "You are my **Son [Jesus]**, and I love You.
> I am very pleased with You."
> Luke 3:22 (NIRV).

Jesus promised to send this same Spirit from the Father to His disciples.

> "I will send the Friend [the **Holy Spirit**] to you from
> the **Father**. He is the **Spirit of truth**, who comes out
> from the **Father**. When the **Friend** comes to help you,
> **He** will be a witness about **Me [Jesus]**."
> John 15:26 (NIV).

THREE People in ONE.

Let's take a closer look at each one.

1. God the Father

We just read this verse, talking about one God, but it also tells us who God is, so let's read it again.

> "One God and **Father of all**, who is
> over all and through all and in all."
> Ephesians 4:6 (NIV).

God is the Father of all.

He is the best Father we could ever have.

God the Father is the best "Dad" ever, and He is the first Person of the Trinity.

God the Father is also the Creator and Ruler of all. He created the whole universe and is the King of all kings.

Everything began with Him, and He is the Ruler of everything.

2. God the Son

God's Son is Jesus. He is the second Person of the Trinity.

1. God the Father.
2. God the Son.

Read this verse.

> "We also know that the **Son of God** (Jesus) has come.
> And we belong to the true God by belonging to **His
> Son, Jesus Christ**. He is the true God and eternal life."
> 1 John 5:20 (NIV).

Jesus is called the S __ __ of God.

Read this verse.

> "The Son [Jesus] is the **exact likeness** of God,
> who can't be seen."
> Colossians 1:15 (NIRV).

And Jesus is the "E __ __ __ __ likeness" of God the
Father.

Jesus is equal to God. Jesus is God.
Jesus is equal to God, but He had a different job to do.

God sent His Son, Jesus, to earth to be born as a baby. He became a man and walked on earth, just like we do. He was born, like us, lived, and then died.

Read this verse.

> "The Word [Jesus] **became a human being.**
> He made His home with us."
> John 1:14 (NIV).

God the Father sent His Son, **Jesus**, into the world to die for us.

- Jesus was sent to do God's will.

- He was sent to be our Savior.

- He was sent to earth to pay our sin penalty and to die in our place.

Read this verse.

> "For **God [the Father]** so loved the world that He gave His one and only **Son [Jesus]**, that whoever believes in Him shall not perish but have eternal life."
> John 3:16 (NIV).

3. God the Holy Spirit.

God is also the Holy Spirit.

The Holy Spirit is the third "Person" of the Trinity.

1. God the Father.
2. God, the Son.
3. God, the Holy Spirit.

Read this verse.

> "These are the things
> God has revealed to us by **His Spirit**."
> 1 Corinthians 2:10 (NIV).

The Holy Spirit "R __ __ __ __ __ __" things to us.

God, the Holy Spirit is the Comforter and Counselor. He helps us follow God and do His will.

He teaches us and reminds us to do the right things.

The Holy Spirit is probably the least known to us, but He is equally important.

We will talk some more about the Holy Spirit when we answer the next question.

The Bible tells us that the three Persons of God all work together.

Each Person has a different job.

Each Person is equally God, working together perfectly to achieve God's plan, with no one Person having a different agenda or will.

It's confusing, I know.

Let's take a closer look.

Trying to Understand

The Trinity (three Persons in one) might be the hardest thing to understand.

Some people have tried to explain the Trinity in these five ways.

1. The Trinity is Like an Egg.

One egg has three different parts: the shell, the white, and the yoke.

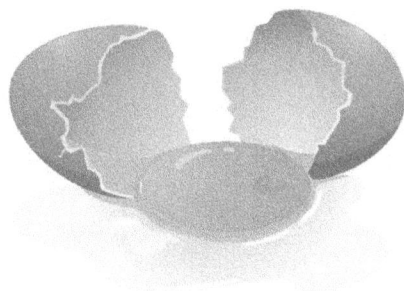

2. The Trinity is like an apple.

ONE apple has three different parts – the skin, the flesh, and the seed.

An egg and an apple might be helpful ways to try to understand this mystery, but they are not perfect.

Why not?

Comparing the three members of the Trinity to an apple or an egg makes it seem like each "Person" is just like three different and unequal parts of God with the same nature.

Each piece of the egg and apple is not complete without the other parts.

- The egg is not a complete egg without a yolk.
- The apple is not a full apple without the core.

The pieces of the egg (shell, yolk, white) and the apple (skin, seeds, apple flesh) don't share the same nature.

- The egg white is different from the yolk and the shell.
- The skin of the apple is made of different materials than the apple seeds and the flesh.

The parts of an egg and an apple are not equal.

- Imagine if you wanted an egg but were just given the shell.

- Or imagine if you wanted to eat an apple, but all that you were given was the core.

With God, each Person is complete on their own. God the Father, God the Son, and God the Holy Spirit are equal. They are each 100% completely God.

3. The Trinity is like a Three-Leaf Clover

A three-leaf clover has THREE different leaves coming together to make ONE clover.

Each leaf is basically equal and made of the same things as the other leaves.

But a three-leaf clover is not a good example for the Trinity because each of the three leaves is only a 'part' of the clover.

One leaf is not fully the "clover" without the other two leaves.

God is not divided into three parts.

- The Son isn't one-third God.

- The Holy Spirit isn't one-third God.
- God the Father isn't one-third God.

Each person of the Trinity is fully God, all on their own.

4. The Trinity is Like Water.

Water can come in three different forms. It can be a liquid (to drink), a solid (ice), or a gas (steam).

Water can be in different states, yet it is actually made of the same thing (H_2O).

- Our glass of water is 100% water.
- Ice is 100% water.
- Steam is 100% water.

The problem when trying to compare water to God is that water can't exist as a solid, a liquid, and a gas at the same time.

God doesn't change, so that sometimes He's the Father, sometimes He's the Son, and other times the Holy Spirit.

He is ONE God and THREE persons **all at once!**

5. The Trinity is like the Celtic Trinity Knot

The Celtic Trinity Knot has three distinct loops in the design.

Try to trace the loops of the knot with a pen. Did you notice that when you traced the loop pattern, there was no beginning or end? It's all one connected line!

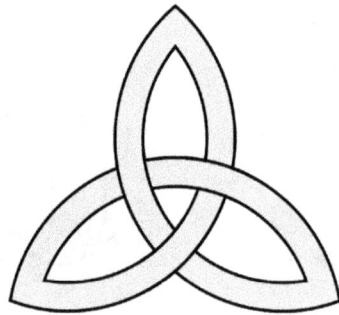

The center of the knot reminds us that God is ONE God. The loops remind us that God is also THREE Persons.

The Celtic knot is a man-made, physical, created object; a symbol. God is not a physical object or symbol. But it is probably the best illustration of what God is like.

The Trinity? Confusing? Yes!

There is really no way to explain it
.

Will you be able to understand better when you get older?

Not really, because our brains cannot fully understand an infinite, invisible, immeasurable God.

Read this verse.

> "Do you know how **deep the mysteries** of God are?
> Can you discover the limits
> of the Mighty One's knowledge?"
> Job 11:7 (NIV).

The answer to the question in that verse is "no." We cannot discover the limit to God's knowledge because there is no limit.

God is so great. We will never be able to understand everything about Him.

But that's what makes Him GOD!

Read this verse.

> "How great God is!
> **We'll never completely understand Him.**"
> Job 36:26 (NIRV).

UNDERSTANDING GOD

We can get to know God, but we will never be able to understand Him.

He is the Creator of the earth, the almighty King of Kings.

It's impossible for us to wrap our human minds around the God of the world.

No one fully understands everything. It comes down to "belief" and "trust."

Big Questions

1. What is God Like?
2. How Did God Create the World?
3. Who Created God?
4. How Can Jesus Be God, But Also God's Son?
5. Who is the Holy Spirit?

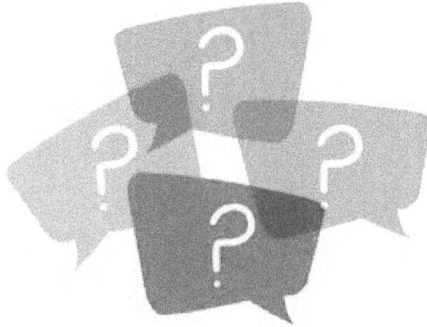

5. Who is the Holy Spirit?

It's hard to understand everything about God.
It's even more difficult to understand the Holy Spirit.

We don't talk about the Holy Spirit as much as we do about Jesus and God the Father. I think because He is more difficult to figure out.

The Holy Spirit is equal with God the Father and God the Son

He is a Spirit, but not like the "spirits" that we think of. Some people call Him the Holy Ghost, but He is not a ghost.

He has a will, and He can think and speak.
He is a Person.

We need Him as much as we need God the Father and God the Son.

The Holy Spirit is God, just like Jesus and God the Father are.

Let's read what the Bible has to say about Him.

1. The Holy Spirit is a Person

We already talked about this a bit, but let's look a little closer.

The Bible tells us that the Holy Spirit is a person, and it tells us a lot about Him.

The Holy Spirit Can Be Resisted.

We can choose to disobey the Holy Spirit's commands.

Read this Bible verse.

> "You stubborn people! You won't obey! You won't listen! You are just like your people of long ago! **You always oppose the Holy Spirit!**"
> Acts 7:51 (NIRV).

Fill in the blanks.

We can O __ __ __ __ __ the Holy Spirit.

We can fight against what He wants.

The Holy Spirit Can Be Sad.

When people refuse to obey what the Holy Spirit is telling them, it makes Him sad. We can also make Him sad by what we do and say.

Read these verses.

> "Yet they rebelled and **grieved His Holy Spirit**."
> Isaiah 63:10 (NIV).

> "And **do not grieve** the Holy Spirit of God."
> Ephesians 4:30 (NIV).

We can G __ __ __ __ __ the Holy Spirit.

We can cause the Holy Spirit to be sad and hurt when we disobey Him.

He feels disappointed when we refuse to obey.

The Holy Spirit Can Be Disrespected.

Read this Bible verse.

> "They also include people who have **disrespected the Holy Spirit** who brings God's grace."
> Hebrews 10:29 (NIV).

We can disrespect the Holy Spirit by ignoring Him, just the same as we can disrespect other people.

We can ignore Him.
We can disobey Him.
We can refuse to do what He says.

He is a person!

2. The Holy Spirit is a Friend.

When we trust in Jesus to save us, the Holy Spirit comes to live within us. He is like a bridge between God and us.

The Bible says the Holy Spirit is our "friend."

Read this Bible verse.

> **"I will send the Friend** [the Holy Spirit] to you from the Father. He is the Spirit of truth, who comes out from the Father. When the **Friend** comes to help you, He will be a witness about me."
> John 15:26 (NIRV).

The Holy Spirit is a "F __ __ __ __ __.

We cannot see Jesus with our eyes as the disciples could in the New Testament, but God sent the Holy Spirit to be with us instead.

He came to help us.
He came to be our friend.

Read this Bible verse.

"I will ask the Father. And He will give you another **Friend** to help you and to be with you forever. That **Friend is the Spirit** of truth. The world can't accept Him. That's because the world does not see Him or know Him. But you know Him. He lives with you, and He will be in you... **the Friend is the Holy Spirit**."
John 14:16-17 (NIRV).

The Holy Spirit is a Friend.

He Loves Us.

Read this Bible verse.

"Pray for me with **the love the Holy Spirit provides**."
Romans 15:30 (NIRV).

He Helps Us When We Are Weak.

The Holy Spirit helps us and promises to be with us forever.

Read this Bible verse.

"In the same way,
the Holy Spirit **helps us** when we are weak."
Romans 8:26 (NIRV).

"I [Jesus] will ask the Father. And He will give you
[believers] another Friend **to help you**
and to be with you forever."
John 14:16–17 (NIRV).

The Holy Spirit Helps Us to Pray.

There will be many times when we are hurting, and we don't know how or what to pray. The Holy Spirit promises to help us pray.

Read this Bible verse.

"We don't know what we should pray for.
But **the Spirit Himself prays for us**."
Romans 8:26 (NIRV).

The Holy Spirit Prays for Us.

The Bible tells us that the Holy Spirit not only helps us to pray, but He also prays for us.

Read this Bible verse.

"And the **Spirit prays for God's people**
just as God wants Him to pray."
Romans 8:27 (NIRV).

The Holy Spirit Gives Gifts.

The Holy Spirit also gives us special gifts so that we can help other people.

Read this Bible verse.

> "**He gives gifts** to each person, just as He decides."
> 1 Corinthians 12:11 (NIRV).

The Holy Spirit is our friend. He is always there in the background, loving us, praying for us, and helping us whenever we need.

We need to ask for the Holy Spirit to help us every day.

And He will.

3. The Holy Spirit is a Teacher.

The Holy Spirit Teaches Us.

The Holy Spirit helps us to understand the Bible when we read it, so we can understand what God is trying to say to us.

> "But the Advocate, the Holy Spirit,
> whom the Father will send in My name,
> **will teach you all things** and will remind
> you of everything I have said to you."
> John 14:26 (NIV).

Sometimes, I get great ideas that I would never have thought of on my own. I know that they are from the Holy Spirit, teaching me what to do.

The Holy Spirit Speaks to Us.

The Holy Spirit is God's voice to us, telling us how to obey and best live our lives.

> "While they were worshiping the Lord
> and fasting, **the Holy Spirit spoke.**
> "Set apart Barnabas and Saul for me."
> Acts 13:2 (NIRV).

The Holy Spirit Knows What We're Thinking and What We're Doing.

> **"The Holy Spirit knows everything**
> you're thinking and everything you do."
> Acts 13:2 (NIRV).

The Holy Spirit is With Us Always.

When Jesus rose from the dead, He left earth and returned to be with His Father in heaven.

God sent the Holy Spirit to be with us always.

- You can ask the Holy Spirit to help whenever you need a friend.

- You can ask the Holy Spirit to help whenever you feel weak.

- You can ask the Holy Spirit to help whenever you don't understand.

You can pray and ask the Holy Spirit for help when you are confused or unsure. He will be there for you!

Let's look at a chapter in the book of John that teaches us about the Holy Spirit.

Read John 16:4-6.

Jesus was explaining to His disciples why He must leave and return to heaven. The disciples were sad and didn't understand.

> "I did not tell you this from the beginning because I was with you, but now **I am going to Him** who sent Me. None of you asks Me, 'Where are you going?' Rather, **you are filled with grief** because I have said these things.
> John 16:4-6 (NIV).

Jesus had been with them every day for three years.

- Imagine what it must have been like to have Jesus right there with you.

- Imagine being able to hug Him when you were sad.

- Or being able to talk to Him whenever you wanted.

The disciples were sad and confused that Jesus was leaving. They didn't want Him to go.

Jesus was leaving earth and going back to heaven to be with His Father.

What would they do without Him?

Read John 16:7.

"But very truly I tell you, it is for your good that I am going away. Unless I go away, **the Advocate** will not come to you; but if I go, **I will send Him to you**."
John 16:7 (NIV).

An "advocate" is a person who supports you and listens to your fears and doubts. They help you find a way through, helping you find the right path.

The Advocate that Jesus was talking about was the Holy Spirit.

The disciples didn't know who the Holy Spirit was.
So, Jesus spent some time explaining.

Read John 16:8-11.

> "When He [the Holy Spirit] comes, He will prove the
> world to be in the wrong about sin and righteousness
> and judgment: **about sin**, because people do not
> believe in me; **about righteousness,** because I am
> going to the Father, where you can see me no longer;
> **and about judgment**, because the prince of this world
> now stands condemned."
> John 16:8-11 (NIV).

The Holy Spirit would do many things.

The Holy Spirit:

1. Convicts the world of **sin** [helps us see our sin].

The Holy Spirit **warns** us when we are tempted to do the
wrong thing. When we feel guilty about something we
have done, that is the Holy Spirit convicting us of our
sins.

2. Teaches about **righteousness** (since Jesus wouldn't be
physically present to do so).

The Holy Spirit **teaches** us about righteousness. That is a
big word that means He will teach us how to live. The
Holy Spirit will guide us in the way that we should go.

3. Reminds people of the coming judgment.

The Holy Spirit **reminds** us how everything ends. If we trust in Jesus to save us, we will not be judged. The prince of the world (Satan), however, will stand condemned and be judged forever.

Read John 16:13.

The Holy Spirit works in our hearts to guide our thinking.

> "But when He, the Spirit of truth, comes,
> **He will guide you** into all the truth."
> John 16:13 (NIV).

Fill in the blanks.

The Holy Spirit G __ __ __ __ __ us.

Jesus leaving earth and returning to heaven changed everything for the disciples.

The Holy Spirit was coming in His place, but they didn't understand how that would change things.

After teaching the disciples about the Holy Spirit, Jesus asked the disciples the big question.

Read the rest of John 16:13.

> "Do you now believe?"
> John 16:31 (NIV).

Jesus finishes by asking a question.

"Do you now B __ __ __ __ __ __?

Believing in Jesus is the most important thing.

- Do you believe?
- Do you trust Me?

Life is difficult, but Jesus asks us to believe and trust Him.

We Can Trust in God.

Do you trust God?

Sometimes trusting and believing are hard, especially when things don't go the way we want them to.

There is an interesting story in the Bible about a father whose son couldn't speak and kept having seizures. The father was very concerned, so he brought his son to Jesus, hoping that Jesus would heal him.

Jesus told the man,

> "Everything is possible for one **who believes**."
> Mark 9:23 (NIV).

How much is possible with God?

E _ _ _ _ _ _ _ _ _.

The man replied:

> "I do believe. **Help me overcome my unbelief!**"
> Mark 9:24 (NIV).

Do you ever feel like this?
I do.

I believe God, but then I wonder.

I know that God is good and wants the best for me. But when those really hard times come, there is still that tiny part that doubts.

- Is God really there?
- Does He really know?
- Will He really help?

God asks us to believe, but also understands that we sometimes struggle.

The Holy Spirit will help us believe.

The story ends with this encouragement.

Read this verse.

> "I have told you these things so that in Me you may have peace. In this world, you will have trouble. **But take heart! I have overcome the world."**
> John 16:33 (NIV).

We CAN trust God.
We can have peace in the middle of trouble.

Why?
Because Jesus has already won the fight!

UNDERSTANDING GOD

Jesus won the victory over death.
He died, and then He rose again.
Jesus overcame the world.

We are in good hands! Just TRUST!

Big Questions

1. What is God Like?
2. How Did God Create the World?
3. Who Created God?
4. How Can Jesus Be God, but Also God's Son?
5. Who is the Holy Spirit?
6. Why Does God Let Bad Things Happen?

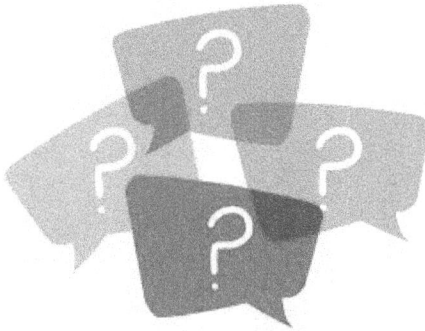

6. Why Does God Let Bad Things Happen?

Sometimes, we struggle to understand why God allows certain things to happen.

If God is love, then…

- Why did I get sick?
- Why did my friend die?
- Why did my parents get divorced?

There are SO many natural disasters, violence, and disease.

- Hurricanes, earthquakes, tornadoes, fires, and floods.
- Wars and crime and all of the consequences.
- Poverty, famine, and hunger.

If God is all-powerful and can stop these bad things from happening, why does God allow so much suffering?

That's a really hard question!

We all want to know, "Why?"

If God is as powerful as the Bible says, He could stop them all, couldn't He?

If God is in control of everything, then He could fix it all, couldn't He?

The truth is that we were not created for this world.
We were created for heaven.

He created the world as a perfect place, but Adam and Eve disobeyed God.

Their sin changed everything.
It introduced sickness, pain, and death into the world.

We are sinners, just like Adam and Eve, and we live in a world that has been affected by sin. We all face trouble and pain.

Read this Bible verse.

> "My brothers and sisters,
> **you will face all kinds of trouble."**
> James 1:2–4 (NIV).

Fill in the blanks.
The Bible tells us that we will face T __ __ __ __ __ __.

For now, the sin of the world results in natural disasters, violence, and disease. God allows the consequences of sin in the world.

When we experience those consequences, we know three things.

1. God is in control.

The trials we face will never be more than we can handle. God will always provide a way out.

> "No temptation (or testing) has overtaken you except what is common to mankind.
> And God is faithful; **He will not let you be tempted beyond what you can bear.**
> But when you are tempted, He will also provide a way out so that you can endure it."
> 1 Corinthians 10:13 (NIV).

God promises that we will not be tempted more than we can bear.

He also promises to provide a W __ __ O __ __.

When we are tempted to do the wrong thing, there is always a way to fight that temptation.

God is F __ __ __ __ __ __ __.

He WILL help us.

2. God promises to be with us.

Whatever suffering comes our way, we can be sure that God is with us.

He will never leave us.

> "The Lord Himself goes before you and will be with you; **He will never leave you nor forsake you**. Do not be afraid; do not be discouraged."
> Deuteronomy 31:8 (NIV).

God will never L _ _ _ _ you.

God will never F _ _ _ _ _ _ you.

He will never disappoint you or let you down.

You have no reason to be afraid.

3. **Our pain is never wasted.**

Our pain is for a purpose.
It is never wasted.

Even in the most tragic of situations, we can know that all things work together for good.

The Bible tells us that if we love God, He promises that our pain will always have a purpose.

Read this verse.

> "And we know that **in all things God works for the good** of those who love Him."
> Romans 8:28 (NIV).

What does that mean?

- Does it mean that we will get what we want?
  No.

- Does it mean that everything will go the way that we want?
  No.

It means that everything will work out just as God planned it.

Read this verse.

> "For I know the plans I have for you," declares
> the Lord, "**plans to prosper you and not to harm
> you, plans to give you hope and a future.**"
> Jeremiah 29:11 (NIV).

God's plan is to P __ __ __ __ __ you.

To give us H __ __ __ and a F __ __ __ __ __ __.

- Our pain is never wasted. Everything that happens
  here on earth is for a purpose.

- We might not be able to see that purpose yet, but
  one day, we will.

One day, God will make everything right again.

All of the questions we have now will be answered
when we get home to heaven.

In the meantime, we can trust that God is all-powerful,
all-wise, and all-good.

Big Questions

1. What is God Like?
2. How Did God Create the World?
3. Who Created God?
4. How Can Jesus Be God but Also God's Son?
5. Who is the Holy Spirit?
6. Why Does God Let Bad Things Happen?
7. Does God Make Mistakes?

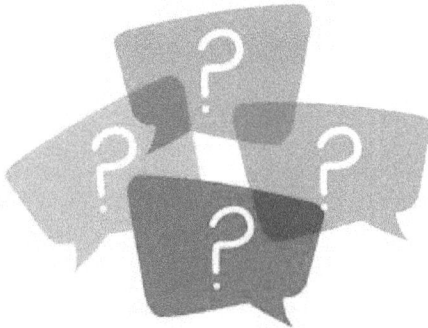

7. Does God Make Mistakes?

We make a lot of mistakes, but God doesn't!

Making mistakes is part of being an imperfect human, and since God isn't human, He doesn't make mistakes.

Read this verse.

> "As for God, **His way is perfect.**"
> Psalms 18:30 (NIRV).

Everything that God does is P __ __ __ __ __ __.

It might seem that the world is a disaster, but God has everything under control.

There are no surprises with God.
He knows the future, and everything is going just as He planned.

We might not understand, but we can trust that God does.

Read this verse.

> "Great is our Lord. **His power is mighty.**
> **There is no limit to His understanding.**"
> Psalm 147:5 (NIRV).

UNDERSTANDING GOD

There is no L __ __ __ __ to God's understanding.

> "The heavens are higher than the earth.
> And **My ways are higher than your ways**.
> My thoughts are higher than your thoughts."
> Isaiah 55:9 (NIRV).

God's thoughts are WAY H __ __ __ __ __ than ours!

We might not understand why things happen the way they do.

But that's OK.
We are not God!

In the meantime, we must trust.

- Trust that God doesn't make mistakes.

- Trust that God's way is perfect.

- Trust that God's plan is to give us hope and a future.

One day, Jesus is coming back.

And then God will make everything perfect again.

> "He will **wipe away every tear** from their eyes.
> There will be **no more death**. And there will be **no more sadness**. There will be **no more crying or pain**."
> Revelation 21:4 (NIRV).

When Jesus comes back,

- There will be no more T __ __ __ __.

- There will be no more D __ __ __ __.

- There will be no more S __ __ __ __ __ __.

- There will be no more C __ __ __ __ __ or P __ __ __.

Read this verse.

> "Do not let your hearts be troubled.
> You believe in God. Believe in Me also.
> There are **many rooms in My Father's house.**
> If this were not true, would I have told you that I am
> going there? Would I have told you that **I would
> prepare a place for you there?**
> If I go and do that, I will come back. And **I will take
> you to be with Me**. Then you will also be where I am."
> John 14:1-3 (NIRV)

God is preparing a house for us in heaven with many

R __ __ __ __.

God is preparing a special P __ __ __ __ for us right now! And one day, He will come back and take us there!

Sometimes, it's hard to trust that God is good. But remember that He always has a purpose, and He doesn't make mistakes.

Big Questions

1. What is God Like?
2. How Did God Create the World?
3. Who Created God?
4. How Can Jesus Be God but Also God's Son?
5. Who is the Holy Spirit?
6. Why Does God Let Bad Things Happen?
7. Does God Make Mistakes?
8. Does God Love Me?

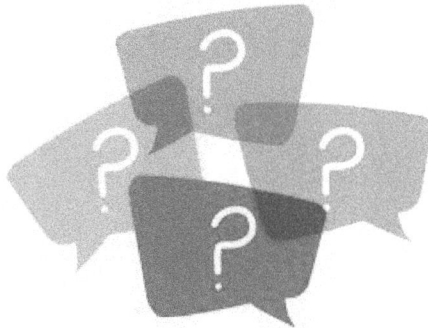

8. Does God Love Me?

This is the most important question of them all.
Does God love me?

The answer is:

YES! YES! YES!

GOD LOVES YOU!

It's the best news of all!
The God of the universe loves you.

Can you believe that?
The Creator of the whole world loves you!

Read this Bible verse.

"Dear friends, let us love one another, for **love comes from God**. Everyone who loves has been born of God and knows God. Whoever does not love, does not know God because **God is love**."
1 John 4:7-9 (NIV).

Love comes from G __ __.

God IS L __ __ __.

UNDERSTANDING GOD

God can't help Himself. It is who He is.
He IS love.

If you have trusted in Jesus to save you, then you are a
child of God.

No matter what you've done, you will always be a part of
His family.

Perhaps you are not the best son or daughter, always
getting into trouble. Disobeying or talking back to your
parents.

But nothing can change the fact that you are a part of your
family.

- Your parents will be your parents even if they walk
  out on you.
- You will always be their son or daughter, no
  matter how badly you behave.

You were born into your family, and you will be part of
that family forever.

It's the same with God's family.

Once you trust in Jesus to save you, you become a part of

God's family.

Nothing you do can change that.
Even if you behave badly!

You are a child of God.
You are a child of the King of Kings.

Have you ever wanted to be a prince or princess?
Well, guess what?
You already are!

You are royalty because you belong to the King of all kings!

How much does God love me?

I remember when our children were little, I would spread my arms as wide as they could go and tell them,

"I love you THIS much."

Well, guess what?

God loves us even more than that.

Read this Bible verse.

> "Your love, Lord, **reaches to the heavens,**
> Your faithfulness to the skies."
> Psalm 36:5 (NIV).

God's love reaches all the way to the H __ __ __ __ __ __.

It's not just a little bit of love. It's a whole LOT of love reaching all the way from earth to heaven.

That's a really long way!

And His love lasts forever and ever.

> "Give thanks to the God of heaven.
> **His love endures forever.**"
> Psalm 136:26 (NIV).

God's love E __ __ __ __ __ __ forever.
It never ends.

His love is there when we fail.
His love is there when we sin.

It is there FOREVER!

"Forever" seems like a long time.

- Do you ever feel like you've been waiting in the lunch line at school... forever?

- Do you ever feel like you've been waiting for your birthday... forever?

- Do you ever feel like you've been waiting for Christmas ... forever?

Forever is a long time, but God's love really does last forever! It will never end.

And there's one more thing.

God doesn't just love you.
He LIKES you, too!

> "The Lord your God is with you.
> He is the Mighty Warrior who saves.
> **He will take great delight** in you.
> In **His love**, He will no longer punish you.
> Instead, **He will sing for joy** because of you."
> Zephaniah 3:17 (NIRV).

God takes great D __ __ __ __ __ __ in us!

He S __ __ __ __ for joy because of us.

God REALLY LIKES you!

The Bible also says that God the Father loves us so much
that He made a way for us to be His children.

Read this verse.

> "See what great love **the Father** has lavished on
> us, that we should be called children of God."
> 1 John 3:1 (NIV).

The word "lavished" means "heaped," "poured," or "smothered."

- "I love it when my mashed potatoes have been **smothered** with gravy."
- "I love it when my ice cream is **smothered** in caramel sauce."

Well, God has "smothered" us with His love.

Why? Because He is our Father. We are a part of His family.

He cares for those who have no fathers or wives whose husbands have died. He loves the poor and needy.

Perhaps your dad wasn't the best.
My dad wasn't.

He would yell and hit us.
It was always scary when he came home from work because we never knew what would happen.

If your dad left your family or if he was a bad dad, just remember, you have the very best "Dad" ever.

UNDERSTANDING GOD

God is a Father to everyone who has trusted in Jesus.

And He is the PERFECT Father.

Even though the world doesn't always make sense, God can be trusted to do what is right and good.

The world is confusing and messy, but God has the answers to all of life's questions.

As we read the Bible and learn more about God and His plans for us, we will find a way through the mess.

GOD'S ANSWERS

1. Don't Try to Hide from God.

1. Don't Try to Hide from God.

What should our response be to God?

God doesn't want us to hide from Him.

In fact, we cannot hide from God. It's impossible.

A long time ago, Adam and Eve chose to disobey God. He gave them one command:

> "Do not eat from the Tree of the Knowledge of Good and Evil."

You probably know the end of the story. They ruined everything by disobeying.

After choosing to disobey, they tried to hide from God.

> "Then the man and His wife heard the sound of the Lord God as He was walking in the garden in the cool of the day, and **they hid from the Lord God** among the trees of the garden."
> Genesis 3:8 (NIV).

Adam and Eve immediately knew they had sinned, and they felt ashamed.

So, they hid among the T __ __ __ __.

They felt ashamed because they knew they had disobeyed.

But it is impossible to hide from God.

God's first question to Adam was, "Where are you?"

> "But the Lord God called to the man, "**Where are you?**" He answered, "I heard you in the garden, and I was afraid because I was naked, so I hid."
> Genesis 3:9-10 (NIV).

Do you think that God knew the answer to that question? Of course, He did.

No one can hide from God.

God's second question was, "Have you eaten from the tree?"

> "**Have you eaten from the tree** that I commanded you not to eat from?"
> Genesis 3:11 (NIV).

God knew the answer to that question, too!

Why do you think God asked questions when He already knew the answers?

- He wanted Adam and Eve to be honest with Him.

- He wanted them to admit their sin.

But instead, they lied.

Who did Adam blame?

> "The man said, "**The woman You put here with me—
> she gave me some fruit** from the tree, and I ate it."
> Genesis 3:12 (NIV).

He blamed the W __ __ __ __.

Who did Eve blame?

> "The woman said,
> "**The serpent deceived me**, and I ate."
> Genesis 3:13 (NIV).

She blamed the S __ __ __ __ __ __.

Neither of them admitted what they did wrong.
They foolishly thought that they could hide from God.

Read this verse.

> "Who can hide in secret places
> so that I cannot see them? declares the Lord."
> Jeremiah 23:24 (NIV).

Can we hide from God? (Circle one).

YES	NO	Not Sure

Trying to hide from God and blame others for our sins is a lost cause.

It doesn't work.
It means that you continue to feel shame.

God just wants us to be honest.

GOD'S ANSWERS

1. Don't Try to Hide from God.
2. Be Honest with God.

2. Be Honest with God.

God wants you to talk with Him about your sins. He already knows all about it, but He wants to hear it from you.

- Share your feelings. Tell Him how you feel.

- Admit your struggles.

- Talk to Him when you feel tempted to do the wrong thing.

You can be honest with God, and He will still love you. When we do, God can step in and help us.

Read these verses.

> "Trust in Him at all times, you people;
> **pour out your hearts to Him,** for God is our refuge."
> Psalm 62:8 (NIV).

The Bible tells us to P __ __ __ out our hearts.

God wants you to be honest with Him about your feelings, struggles, sins, and questions.

- If you're angry, tell Him.

- If you're sad, it's OK to cry out to Him.

He already knows, anyway.

> "You have searched me, Lord, and **You know me**.
> You know when I sit and when I rise;
> **You perceive my thoughts** from afar.
> Psalm 139:1-2 (NIV).

God only wants what is best for you, so don't try to hide.
Be honest.

GOD'S ANSWERS

1. Don't Try to Hide from God.
2. Be Honest with God.
3. Trust God

3. Trust God

God wants us to trust Him.

He chose us to belong to Him.

Read this verse.

> "**God chose us to belong to Christ** before the world was created. **He chose us to be holy and without blame** in His eyes. He loved us."
> Ephesians 1:4 (NIRV).

God chose us to be H __ __ __ and without B __ __ __ __.

But we are sinners.

Read this verse.

> "For **all have sinned** and fall short of the glory of God."
> Romans 3:23 (NIV).

How many of us have sinned?

A __ __ of us.

And there is more bad news.

Read this verse.

> "For the **wages of sin is death**, but the gift of
> God is eternal life in Christ Jesus our Lord."
> Romans 6:23 (NIV).

The penalty for sin is D __ __ __ __.

Sin brought the horrible consequences of death and suffering.

We all deserve to die.

The good news is that God loved us so much that He sent His only Son, Jesus, to die in our place.

Read this verse.

> "**For God so loved the world that He gave** His
> one and only Son, that whoever believes in Him
> shall not perish but have eternal life."
> John 3:16 (NIV).

Jesus paid our sin penalty and died in our place.

If we B __ __ __ __ __ __ in Him, we will have

E __ __ __ __ __ __ L __ __ __.

Believing in Jesus is the same as trusting Him.

- You must believe that you can't get to heaven by your own efforts and good works.

- You must believe that Jesus died for you.

- You must trust that His death paid the full penalty for your sins.

Once you trust in Jesus to save you, your sins are forgiven, and you can know for sure that you will go to heaven one day to be with Him.

In the meantime, God wants us to live for Him.

> "And now, Israel,
> what is the Lord your God asking you to do?
> **Honor him. Live exactly as He wants you to live.**
> **Love him. Serve Him with all your heart and with**
> **all your soul. Obey the Lord's commands and rules.**
> I'm giving them to you today for your own good."
> Deuteronomy 10:12-13 (NIRV).

He wants us to H __ __ __ __ Him.

He wants us to L __ __ __ exactly as He wants you to live.

He wants us to L __ __ __ Him.

He wants us to S __ __ __ __ Him with all of our hearts.

And He wants us to O __ __ __ Him.

And one day, Jesus will return to bring you to heaven.

He will make a new heaven and earth for believers to enjoy forever, free from sin and suffering!

That is the BEST news ever!

UNDERSTANDING GOD

Congratulations

You have completed "UNDERSTANDING GOD."

Write your name and date on your certificate, and have your parent or a teacher sign it for you.

Certificate of Completion
Awarded to

_____

On _____ _____ _____
          Month   Day   Year

For completing UNDERSTANDING GOD.

Presented by _____
                        Signature

Note to Parents

Most parents want to do the right thing, but so often, they are either too busy or overwhelmed. You need to be a good role model to set an example for your children. They are watching.

Here are some suggestions to get you started.

- Make sure your children have a Bible of their own. Make sure it's age-appropriate. They can't read it if they don't understand it (see the following page recommendations).

- Provide notebooks for each child to write down what they learn. Encourage them to write down their prayer requests and the answers to their prayers.

- Encourage them to read their Bible for five minutes every day. We suggest that you begin with the book of John.

- Encourage them to write down any questions and ask you or their Sunday School teacher.

- Make time each day to read your own Bible. Kids learn by watching you. Set a good example for them to follow.

Choosing The Best Bible for Your Child

Here are some recommendations for Bibles to help your kids get excited about God's Word!

MAKE AN AGE-APPROPRIATE CHOICE.
If you want your children to enjoy reading the Bible, buy one that is easy to read, attractive, and engaging. Too often, kids struggle to look up verses at church in a Bible that has tiny print, is in a hard-to-read translation, and has no pictures or illustrations to draw them in.

Paul wrote to young Timothy,

> "And how **from childhood** you have been acquainted with the sacred writings, which are able to make you wise for salvation through faith in Christ Jesus."
> 2 Timothy 3:15 (NIV).

Timothy began studying the Bible as a young child. As parents, we want our kids to know and love God's Word, so buy them a Bible that they will understand.

BUY A BIBLE FOR EACH CHILD

Each child needs their own copy of the Bible. As parents, we spare no expense to buy our kids whatever they need to succeed in school or sports. Do the same for God's Word. Buy them a Bible that they will love to read.

The New International Version for Young Readers (NIrV), the New International Version (NIV), or the English Standard Version (ESV) are good translations for kids. It's one of the most important investments you can make in your child's Christian education and spiritual development.

RECOMMENDED BIBLES FOR CHILDREN

Here are some examples of recommended Bibles available today.

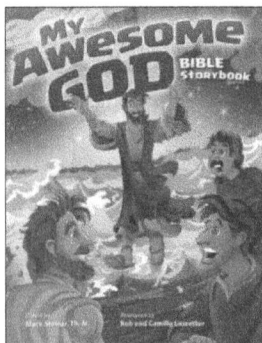

PRESCHOOL
My Awesome God Storybook
The MY AWESOME GOD Storybook Bible is ideal for parents who want to read the key stories of the Bible to their young children. This Bible includes a topical index and helpful discussion questions.

YOUNGER ELEMENTARY
NIrV Adventure Bible for Early
Readers – For Ages 5–10
This is a simpler version of the
children's NIV Bible created for
younger readers.

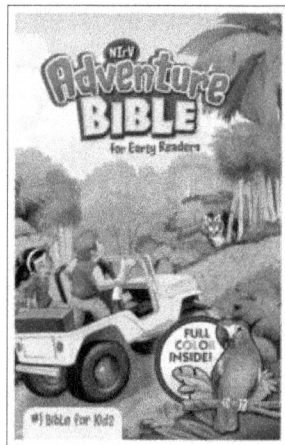

One of the easiest translations is
the New International Reader's
Version (NIrV). The NIrV is the
young reader's edition of this fun,
interactive Bible that helps children learn about what they
are reading through helpful information presented
throughout.

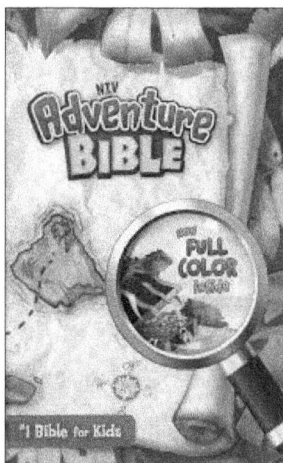

NIV Adventure Bible –
For Ages 8–11
The bestselling NIV Adventure
Bible® will get kids excited about
reading the Scriptures! Your kids
will be captivated by the full-color
features that make it fun and
engaging to read the Bible and
memorize their favorite verses.

CSB Explorer Bible

This Bible reads similarly to the NCV translation and is filled with fun activities, maps, and images that your kids will not want to put down.

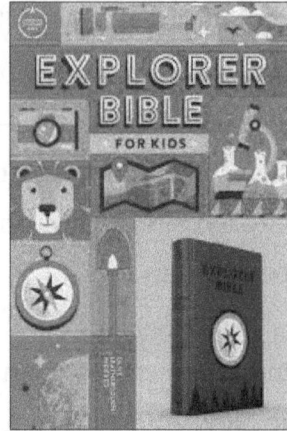

UPPER ELEMENTARY

Your preteen children can really start to master the Word of God! Here are some exciting options!

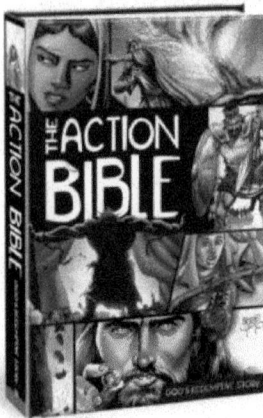

The Action Bible

The Action Bible presents the entire Bible in cool comic book illustrations. Kids will read it cover to cover many times over.

The Action Bible Study Bible
The creators of the Action Comic
Bible also published a Study Bible
edition in both the NIV and ESV.

The Action Study Bible is the
complete text of the Bible, with
select illustrations from the Action
Bible throughout.

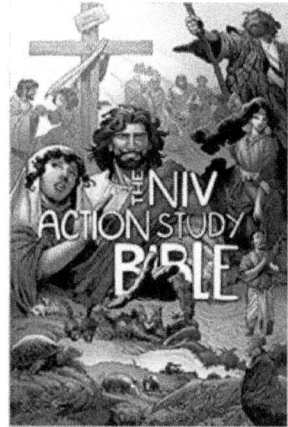

The Understanding Life Series.

UNDERSTANDING SALVATION is a short workbook designed for children ages 7-12 to use independently or with a parent.

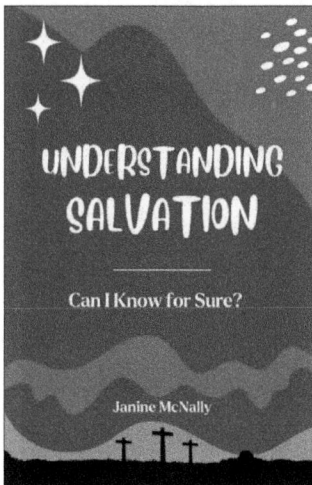

It presents the good news of Jesus in a clear and easy-to-understand way that will help them know FOR SURE that they will live with Jesus in heaven one day.

Children will learn the key principles of salvation, teaching the "Bad News" (sin) and "Good News" (Jesus), along with Bible verses and simple illustrations.

This 120-page book will help them deepen their understanding of God's grace and begin their relationship with Him.

UNDERSTANDING BAPTISM is a 95-page workbook designed for children ages 8-12 to use independently or with a parent or leader.

It is intended for those who have already expressed their belief in Jesus for salvation and have asked about being baptized.

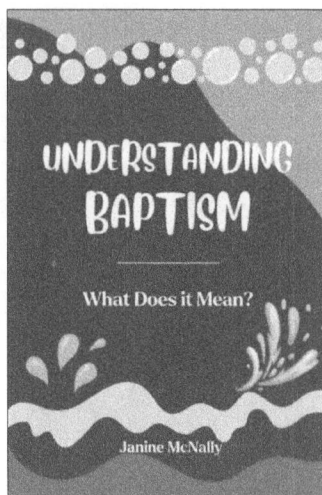

This book answers these questions.

- How can we be saved?
- Can I be sure I am saved?
- What is baptism?
- Why should I be baptized?
- When should I be baptized?
- What happens during a baptism?

UNDERSTANDING GOD is the third book in the "Understanding Life" series for Kids, written for children ages 9-12.

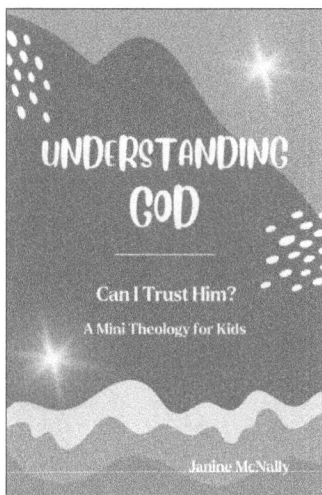

Children are asking questions every day about God, the Bible, salvation, life, death, the afterlife, angels, demons, and more.

We need to be prepared with answers, or they will look elsewhere.

This 135-page book answers the following questions.

1. What is God like?
2. How did He create the world?
3. Who Created God?
4. Who is the Holy Spirit?
5. How can Jesus be God but also be God's Son?
6. Why does God let bad things happen?
7. Can God make mistakes?
8. Does God Love Me?

This book can be used as a training resource for your volunteers or as a parent.

UNDERSTANDING the BIBLE is the fourth book in the series.

When your child asks the tough questions, do you have answers for them? Do they know how to read the Bible and apply it in their lives?

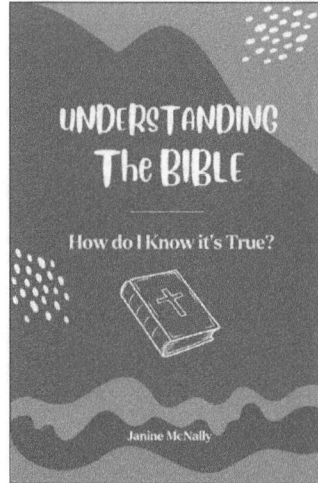

- How do we know the Bible is true?
- Is the Bible trustworthy?
- How do we know that it is really God's Word?

Written for children ages 8-12, this 120-page book teaches some basic Bible apologetics.

The content includes:
Three Big Words:
1. Inspiration - Written by God and Man
2. Inerrancy - No mistakes
3. Preservation

The Bible's Structure
How to Have a Quiet Time
How to Memorize God's Word

UNDERSTANDING ME addresses the big question, "Who am I?" in this 120-page book for kids ages 9-12.

Our world says, "There's no right or wrong," "We decide what is true and right," and "We can create our own identity."

At a time when kids are going through enormous changes, they are confronted with ambiguity and confusion.

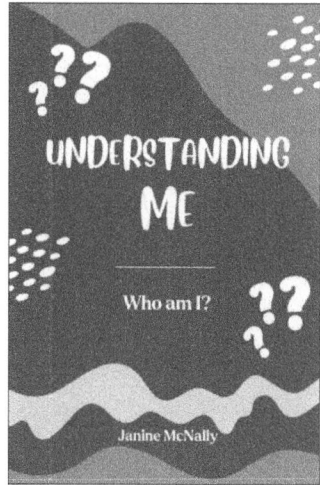

1. Who am I?
2. Am I loved?
3. Am I alone?
4. Why am I here?

Each question is handled from a Biblical perspective and ends with the hope of a new life, a new body, and a new world for those who have trusted in Jesus.

UNDERSTANDING HARD QUESTIONS is the sixth book in the "Understanding Life" series for kids.

It answers 56 of the most common questions asked by kids from a Biblical perspective and in an age-appropriate way.

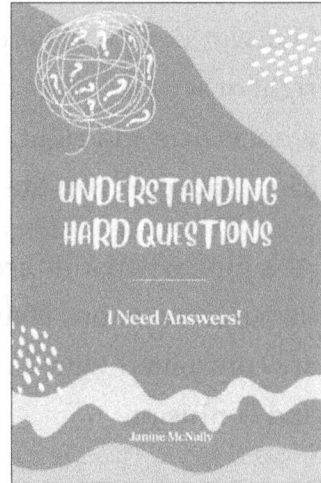

- Who created God?
- Does God speak to people?
- Will God stop loving me if I keep sinning?
- How did Jesus perform miracles?
- Why do people get sick and die?
- Why did my parents get divorced?
- Can Christians lose their salvation?
- How can God forgive murderers?
- Why is sex outside of marriage wrong?
- Are there more than two genders?
- Can I be sure that I will go to heaven?

Written for kids ages 9-12, this 165-page book answers these questions using basic Bible apologetics.

UNDERSTANDING LIFE & DEATH is written for children ages 8-12 and addresses the questions that arise when a child experiences the death of a loved one.

- Why Do People Get Sick and Die?
- What Happens After You Die?
- If God Loves Me, Why Did My Dad Die?
- What is Heaven Like?
- Will Everyone Go to Heaven No Matter What They Believe?
- Do People Who Never Hear About Jesus Go to Heaven?
- Is Hell Real?
- How Could a Loving God Send People to Hell?
- Why Did God Create Satan?

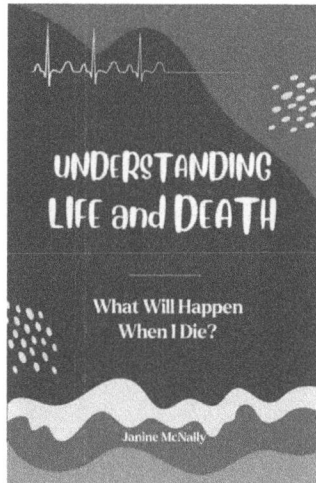

UNDERSTANDING
LIFE and DEATH

What Will Happen
When I Die?

Janine McNally

This 120-page book answers these questions and more from a Biblical perspective in an age-appropriate way. It aims to provide help and hope in times of sadness and grief.

UNDERSTANDING GOD

About the Author

Originally a high school teacher in her native Australia, Janine McNally has partnered with her husband for many years of pastoral ministry.

Janine graduated with a Master of Theology from Dallas Theological Seminary and a Doctor of Ministry from Grace School of Theology.

She is the author of "When You See Fireflies—Equipping Leaders and Parents to Minister Effectively to Generation Alpha," the "Understanding Life for Kids" series, seven devotional books for kids ("10 Minutes with God"), and "STEPS to Knowing Jesus" for kids and preteens.

She passionately believes in reaching kids for Jesus and enlightening leaders and parents about Generation Alpha and beyond.

Janine and Gary have been married for thirty-two years and live in Panama City, Florida.

UNDERSTANDING GOD

They have three grown children, Hannah (married to Kevin), Jonathan (married to Brayton), and Jami Grace.

They also have three beautiful grandchildren, Grayson, Hunter, and Emerson.

About the Ministry

Janine McNally directs the operations of **Equipping Fireflies**, a non-profit dedicated to providing gospel-centered resources that proclaim a message that will grab the attention of this generation, break the magnetic attraction of the increasingly dark world, and lead children to the Light.

THE STORY BEHIND THE NAME

"When do we have to come inside?"
"When you see the fireflies."

Our kids loved to play outside, but as night began to fall, it was time to come in, where it was safe. Each evening, for a short time, the fireflies would light up our entire backyard. Their unmistakable glow was the signal that it was time.

Our world has become much darker. We desperately need the kids and their families to hear the call. "Come inside where it's safe." The world is rapidly becoming bleaker as the generations race by, yet our children are running towards the night.

We must proclaim a message that grabs their attention, one that they understand and that will break the magnetic attraction of the increasingly dark world.

"You are the light of the world.
Let your light shine *before others that they may see your good deeds and glorify your Father in heaven."*
Matthew 5:14; 16

OUR PASSION
Statistics show that most Christians trusted Christ between the ages of 3 and 12. Our passion is to reach children for Jesus and serve, equip, and encourage Children's Ministry leaders and parents.

THE GOOD NEWS
When Jesus died on the cross, He did EVERYTHING that God requires for us to go to heaven when we die."

EQUIPPING FIREFLIES

Lighting the Way for the Next Generations.
www.equippingfireflies.com

"And these words which I command you today shall be in your heart. You shall teach them diligently to your children, and shall talk of them when you sit in your house, when you walk by the way, when you lie down, and when you rise up.
You shall bind them as a sign on your hand, and they shall be as frontlets between your eyes. You shall write them on the doorposts of your house and on your gates."
Deuteronomy 6:6-9

www.ingramcontent.com/pod-product-compliance
Lightning Source LLC
Chambersburg PA
CBHW061733020426
42331CB00006B/1224